the
little
GREEN
BOOK
of Gardening

For Ellen and Maisie, with love and thanks

THIS IS A CARLTON BOOK

Text, illustrations and design copyright © 2008
Carlton Books Limited

This edition published by
Carlton Books Limited 2008
20 Mortimer Street
London W1T 3JW

A CIP catalogue record for this book is available
from the British Library.

ISBN 978-1-84732-065-0

Printed and bound in Singapore

Senior Executive Editor: Lisa Dyer
Senior Art Editor: Gulen Shevki-Taylor
Designer: Emma Wicks
Copy Editor: Nicky Gyopari
Production: Kate Pimm

Your **Carbon Footprint** is the amount of carbon dioxide emitted
due to your daily activities – from washing a load of laundry to
driving to work. See www.carbonfootprint.com for ways to reduce
your impact on the environment.

DIANE MILLIS

the little GREEN BOOK of Gardening

250 TIPS FOR AN ECO LIFESTYLE

CARLTON
BOOKS

Are you up to date on insecticide-free pest control? Do you know the secrets of good composting? Are you working with nature and ecosystems? If you want to garden in an environmentally conscious, organic and sustainable way, then this little book contains 250 practical tips that will set you on the path to becoming a truly 'green' gardener. Not only does responsible gardening enable you to grow food free from chemicals and pesticides, reduce pollution, recycle your food scraps and garden cuttings into crops that will grow more food and create a haven for wildlife, but it will also put you in touch with nature and its cycles, and allow you to contribute to a cleaner global environment.

1 GARDEN ORGANIC

It's not just about rejecting the usual array of pesticides. Organic gardening means buying locally, rejecting genetically modified products, reusing and recycling as much as possible (including water), feeding the soil, nurturing wildlife, avoiding artificial fertilizers, and preserving heritage seeds.

2 KEEP IT GREEN

A green garden can help reduce the impact of climate change on your property. With rainfall and temperatures both predicted to rise, it can soak up sudden downpours and maintain surface temperatures better than paved areas. Researchers have found that adding just 10% to the existing green cover of high-density urban areas can keep maximum surface temperatures below today's levels up until the 2080s.

4 THE BIGGER PICTURE

Green gardening practices also form part of systems or philosophies including permaculture and biodynamic agriculture. Exploring these areas will give you fresh ideas for your garden, and perhaps stimulate an interest in other areas of sustainable living.

3 IT ADDS UP

Your one garden may seem insignificant but one nation's gardens make up a significant amount of vital green space. In the UK alone, an estimated 15 million domestic gardens cover an area greater than all of the designated National Nature Reserves combined.

5 DON'T WASTE YOUR WASTE

If you're not going to compost your garden waste, don't just dump it in with your other trash. Take it to your nearest municipal tip where they will have facilities for it to be collected and composted. Or find out if there's a community composting project in your area that would be happy to take the waste.

6 BE LOW-ENERGY

Resist the urge to put energy-hungry accessories in your garden, such as patio heaters, hot tubs and under-tree lighting. Where once gardens were places for quiet contemplation of the natural world, they have now become extensions to our houses where we expect all the same comforts. Remember that these come at a cost to our climate.

7 PROTECT YOUR SOIL

In nature, it can take around 1,000 years to produce 2.5 cm (1 in) of topsoil so protect your soil with an organic mulch like straw, bark or leaves. This will keep it from being eroded by wind and drying out in the sun. Also, be sure to stockpile and reuse topsoil if you are having work done in the garden.

8 GET OUT AND ABOUT

Organic gardening and farming are increasingly popular so there should be plenty of opportunities for you to visit farms to get inspiration and tips. Contact an organic certifying body such as the Soil Association in the UK or the CSA (Community Supported Agriculture) in the US, or an organic gardening organization, to find them. They may also know of a network of like-minded organic gardeners for you to join.

9 BEWARE THE WORD 'ORGANIC'

Not because organic is bad, but because the use of the word can be. Gardening items that are labelled as 'organic' need only be of living origin – so your organic manure might be from battery chickens. Only those products that are certified as organic by an official certifying body are guaranteed to have been produced under strict organic standards.

10 KEEP YOUR FRONT

Don't be tempted to pave over your front yard. Research has shown that even tiny front gardens or green verges are vital for urban wildlife, and they can house more than 700 different species of insect.

11 REDUCE PAVING

With rainfall predicted to get heavier, paved areas will increase the risk of flash flooding in your area. Plus, water runs off paved areas, picking up pollutants on the way, which often end up in rivers and waterways via storm drains.

12 BE STREET TREE WISE

Don't support tree removal in order to make it easier to park your car. Trees absorb pollution, cool and humidify the air and provide a valuable home for wildlife. On top of all that, in some areas a tree-lined street can add up to 15% to the value of a property.

13 OPT FOR A GREEN DRIVE

If you move your car fairly regularly, then there are plants that will tolerate being parked over. They need to be low-growing and tough enough to withstand occasionally being driven over. Try creeping jenny, bugle and various thymes. Leave planting pockets in paving or gravel to ensure there is soil for them to grow in.

14 DON'T OVERDIG

While turning the soil, breaking up any large clods and digging in compost can help improve soil structure, but there is some evidence that digging too often will have the opposite effect, so give your spade a rest. Instead, spread manure or compost over the surface of the bed and allow the worms to transport the manure deep down into the soil.

15 MAKE COMPOST

Making your own compost is the easiest and best way to give your plants the greatest possible soil. Around 45% of most households' rubbish could actually go straight into a compost bin, which saves the energy needed to collect and process what would otherwise be destined to clog up landfill space.

16 WHAT BELONGS IN A COMPOST BIN

You can toss in all your uncooked fruit and vegetables, lawn clippings and most other garden waste, egg shells, tea bags and coffee filters; also newspaper and cardboard and old cut flowers. Don't add cooked foods, dairy, meat and fish products, cat litter and pet waste, perennial garden weeds and weeds in seed, plastic, glass or aluminium.

17 COMPOSTING KNOW-HOW

Getting to grips with just a few composting 'rules' will give you the best results and lessen the likelihood of bad odours. Make sure you keep your compost so it is moist. Turn the mix occasionally and aim for a mix of 50% greens (wet materials like grass cuttings and fruit and vegetables) and 50% browns (dry items such as cardboard, egg boxes and leaves). If your compost tends to be wet and sludgy, add more browns, but If it's too dry bring in more greens.

18 PLAN YOUR KITCHEN FOR COMPOSTING

You'll be much more likely to keep your vegetable peelings and fruit skins for composting if you have a small container on hand to keep them in. If you are installing a new kitchen, make sure you plan for composting and create space for a bin beneath your main work surface.

19 SPEED UP THE ROT

If it seems as though nothing much is happening in your compost heap, it might need a little help. You can buy organic compost activators and accelerators which contain microorganisms especially cultured for composting. Or you can do it yourself by adding fresh urine to the mix – it is high in nitrogen and can act as a good activator. But you can have too much of a good thing so don't start thinking of your compost as an outdoor lavatory!

20 SOME LIKE IT HOT

A hot compost is the quickest method – it can take just 12 weeks to break down. It can also be beneficial for killing off any weed seeds that might end up in there. For a hot compost fill the compost up in one go, turn the heap every few weeks and chop up tough and bulky material. You can also buy a hot composter that includes an insulating jacket.

21 AVOID PEAT

In the UK and Ireland, over 94% of peatbogs have been damaged or destroyed in order to keep gardeners supplied with peat, which is used as a soil improver, mulch and growing medium. But these bogs are important sites for wildlife and also help absorb carbon dioxide from the atmosphere. It can take from 7,000 to 10,000 years to produce a layer of peat 7–10 m (23–32 ft) thick. In the US, most of the peat comes from Canada, where it is strictly regulated, but it still takes many years for a bog to recover. The message is, don't use peat in your garden.

22 EXPLORE PEAT-FREE ALTERNATIVES

For improving soil and planting, look for peat-free 'multipurpose composts', which include coir-based mixtures, or use your own compost of leaf mould. For mulching, try bark products, cocoa shells, pebbles or cardboard. To increase soil acidity, try pine needles or composted heather or bracken.

23 GET MULCHING

Stop weeds in their tracks, reduce water evaporating from your soil and prevent soil erosion by using a mulch on top of your beds and borders. Organic mulches gradually biodegrade and help soil structure – they include compost, leaves, bark chippings, straw, manure and recycled woodchip. Other mulches include landscape fabric and products made from recycled rubber tyres.

24 CARPET DANGERS

Using carpets as mulch on your vegetable patch, especially if allowed to decompose over time, is not such a good idea. Many carpets, including those made of natural fibres, are treated with toxic moth repellents and fire retardants. Safer alternatives include cardboard over newspaper, weed control fabrics and permeable mulch matting that can be reused.

25 DON'T USE FERTILIZERS

The manufacture and distribution of artificial nitrogen fertilizers requires large amounts of energy, but some studies estimate that only half the amount of fertilizer is actually used by the plants. The rest can be washed away into rivers and streams, causing pollution. An organic garden should get all its nutrient needs from recycled organic materials such as compost and manure. However, you can buy organic fertilizers to correct major deficiencies.

26 A COMFREY TEA FEED

The herb comfrey can make a valuable liquid feed. Take a tub, fill it with 3 kg (3½ lb) comfrey leaves and 45 litres (95 pints) of water, then leave for three to five weeks – it won't smell too good so keep a lid on it! Strain or use a ladle to remove the resulting liquid, which can be used as a feed for tomatoes, runner or dwarf beans and potatoes.

27 NETTLE METTLE

Nettles make a good liquid feed as well, especially young nettles cut in spring as this is when they have the highest levels of major nutrients. Leave 1 kg (2 lb 3 oz) to steep in 10 litres (21 pints) of water. Cover with a lid and use after two weeks. But don't forget to dilute it first – one part nettle liquid to ten parts water.

28 MAKE LEAF MOULD

Let your autumn leaves rot down to make leaf mould – a good soil improver, lawn conditioner and mulch. You can use all sorts of leaves but avoid evergreen leaves such as holly, laurel or Leyland cypress and other conifers as they take much longer to decay. Keep them in tied black plastic sacks (with a few holes in the side) or a wire mesh leaf mould bin, or buy a loose-weave jute sack that will biodegrade. Leaves are slower to rot than other compost items, taking a year or two, so are best recycled separately.

29   ASK FOR LEAVES

As well as collecting fallen leaves from your garden and pavements to make leaf mould, try asking your local authority for leaves that have been collected from parks and cemeteries. Or why not arrange a leaf-gathering event at your local school or community woodland? Avoid those collected from roads, which may contain unwanted contaminants.

30   RAISE YOUR PH WITH EGGS

The ground limestone used by organic gardeners to add lime to their soil requires large amounts of fossil fuel to quarry, grind and transport. Instead, add egg shells (local organic, of course) to your compost heap and spread the compost over your soil.

31

KNOW YOUR MANURE

While animal manure can be a great way to improve your soil, it is essential that you check where it's coming from. Manure from a non-organic farm is likely to be polluted with residues of veterinary products, such as antibiotics that are fed to most intensively reared farm animals on a daily basis, or the remains of toxic worming products. Get your manure from an organic farm or a local source that can provide guarantees regarding its purity.

32

HEAP IT HIGH

To get the best out of your manure you should compost or stack it so that the nutrients in it are stabilized. This also helps break down any harmful residues that it may contain. To stack it, mix the manure with bedding material such as straw and leave, covered, for six months. You may need to leave it for at least a year if wood shavings are the bedding material as they are slow to break down.

33 GROW GREEN MANURES

Rather than leaving your bed empty over winter, grow a green manure. These are plants grown specifically to improve the soil, which are dug back into the soil in early spring. Benefits include: adding nitrogen to the soil by absorbing it from the air and 'fixing' it in their roots, improving soil structure, smothering weeds, protecting soil from heavy rain and preventing nutrients leaching out of the soil into streams and rivers; also providing a home to wildlife. Try clover, alfalfa, mustard, buckwheat and tares.

34 MAKE FRIENDS WITH WORMS

Worms can do the composting for you – 500 g (18 oz) of composting worms will eat about 1–1.5 kg (1¼–3¼ lb) of waste a week. You can buy wormeries (worm bins) or make your own (but don't use garden worms as they won't survive). Either way they require constant warmth, moisture and darkness. A wormery doesn't need much outdoor space either – it will fit on a balcony or even sit indoors.

35 FEED PLANTS WORM TEA

The liquid that comes out of a wormery can be diluted (1 part to 10 parts water) to feed your plants. The rich, crumbly compost can be removed every six months or so from the wormery. Just make sure you pick out the worms and then put them back in with layers of cardboard, a bit of soil and some the kitchen leftovers

36 INSTALL A FOOD DIGESTER

You can recycle all your food, including fish, cooked meat and bones, in a food digester. Digesters, which should be rodent-proof, need to have their base below ground level since over 90% of the waste will be absorbed by the soil as water. Once the digester is full – roughly every two years – the residue can be removed and then dug into the ground.

37 AVOID PESTICIDES AND HERBICIDES

The British public spends around £50 million annually on pesticides such as slug pellets and weed killers, and each year American homeowners apply at least 90 million pounds (40,000 tonnes) of pesticides to their lawns and gardens. These chemicals endanger wildlife and could be putting you and your family's health at risk. A recent study, for example, has found a clear link between two commonly used weed killers and birth defects in children.

38 DISPOSE SAFELY

Don't throw your unwanted pesticides down the drain. A survey has shown that 20–30% of people are doing just that, leading to the contamination of water supplies and the endangering of wildlife in rivers, lakes and groundwater. Just leaving them in the shed isn't a safe solution either because children might be able to reach them. Contact your local authority for advice on where to take your hazardous waste.

39

GET YOUR HANDS DIRTY

You can get rid of many pests with your bare hands. Pick aphids (greenfly) off leaves and drop into soapy water or vegetable oil, or go out at night for a slug or snail blitz. You can make a slug tea with your night-time pickings by leaving the slugs in a bucket of rainwater for a few weeks. The liquid can then be poured over popular slug patches, where it is said to deter them.

40

USE A WATER CANNON

A strong blast of water from a hose will blow many insects off your foliage without having to resort to a single chemical. But try other less water-wasteful methods first.

41 PREPARE THE GROUND

Make sure you reduce the number of hiding places for common pests like slugs and snails. Keep on top of weeding and prune the branches of shrubs lying on the ground. Dig over the soil to bring slugs to the surface and do keep lawn edges trimmed as slugs like to hide under the long grass.

42 BEER DRINKERS

Bury a bowl and fill it with stale beer – it attracts slugs and they will die a boozy death. You can also use grape juice or a tea made from yeast, honey and water. Be sure to keep the lip just above the surface to stop beetles falling in. Slugs, however, will happily climb over.

43 BUG THE SLUGS

Spread the following around your plants to deter or kill slugs: cedar bark or gravel chips, crushed eggshells, herbs (rosemary, lemon balm, wormwood, mint), needles from conifers, seaweed, wood ash, soot and coffee grounds (collect them from your local café or workplace). A sprinkling of bran may also prove effective – although slugs eat the stuff, it swells inside them and kills them.

44 ENCOURAGE NATURAL PREDATORS

Consider introducing ducks, geese and chickens into your garden, and encourage toads to stay by installing a pond and plenty of shady damp areas. Not only will they all enjoy dining on your slugs, but ducks and bantams tend not to damage your plants at the same time.

45 ENLIST LITTLE HELPERS

Children can be surprisingly eager to round up the slugs and snails in a garden. Offer an incentive such as a prize for the biggest creature and your pest-control problems could be over. Should any little ones get the slimy stuff on their fingers, you can remove it with a mixture of warm water and vinegar.

46 LURE THEM IN

Buttered leaves or scooped-out grapefruit halves can be placed around vulnerable crops as a lure for slugs. Remove them by hand when enough have gathered there. You can also clear a bed before planting by placing a heap of cut comfrey leaves on it – clear the leaves and the feeding slugs a few days later at night.

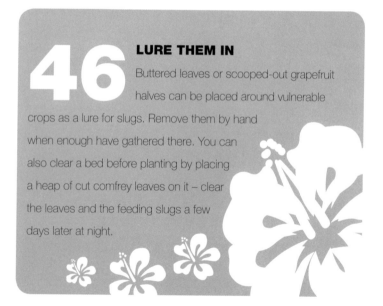

THE BARRIER METHOD

You can buy copper tape, rings and mats, which act as a natural repellent to slugs due to the tiny electrical charge from the metal. Eco-friendly recycled boards that give individual protection to each plant for three weeks are also worth a try. They are impregnated with salt and sulphate, so a slug- and snail-repelling ring forms around the top of the 'wall'.

SEND FOR THE NEMATODES

You can buy nematodes from mail order catalogues or the internet. They are microscopic worms that enjoy nothing more than eating some of the worst enemies in your garden – slugs, vine weevils, chafer grubs and leatherjackets. Sachets of them can be sent through the post and refrigerated, then applied to the soil provided it is at least 5°C (41°F).

WISE UP ON PESTS

Get to know your adversary's habits and you are on the way to beating them. Carrot fly, for example, are attracted to the scent of the carrot. Thin out your seedlings in the evenings when the carrot fly is not about and ensure that any soil disturbed is firmed back down with your hand – carrot fly lay their eggs in loose soil around the seedlings.

BRING IN THE LADIES

Ladybirds (ladybugs) – both adults and larvae – eat most types of aphids and you can now buy them in. One pack of 250 larvae can cover approximately 40 sq m (50 sq yds) and is a particularly good way of introducing ladybirds, especially in existing aphid colony infestations in greenhouses, and also in outdoor areas as they will remain local until they become adults. Adult ladybirds can lay many eggs, so helping to continue the colony of pest control.

51 STICK IT UP

Use dry sticky traps to monitor flying pests. Yellow traps are useful for attracting aphids, whitefly and leafminers. Blue traps are more attractive to thrips. To monitor the extent of pest invasion hang traps above the plants in your greenhouse. Stickier traps can be used for obliterating them.

52 GO EASY WITH ORGANIC PESTICIDES

As a last resort, there is a small range of pesticides and fungicides available to organic gardeners, such as pyrethrum and insecticidal soap, but these should be avoided if possible. They are still poisonous and can harm wildlife beyond the intended target.

53

MAKE YOUR OWN INSECTICIDE

Boiling rhubarb leaves releases oxalic acid, which can kill leaf-eating insects such as cabbage caterpillars and aphids. Boil about 1.3 kg (3 lb) of rhubarb leaves in about 1.7 litre (3 pints) of water for about 15 or 20 minutes. Cool, strain, and mix with soap flakes before spraying on plants. Take care as rhubarb leaves are poisonous to humans if ingested; they are fine on the ground however as the poison breaks down when the leaves are decomposed.

54

MIX WHAT YOU GROW

Mixing flowering plants with your vegetable and fruit plants encourages pest predators such as parasitic wasps, hoverflies and lacewings, the adults of which feed on the nectar from the flowers.

55 TRY COMPANION PLANTING

Get to know which plants can help others by being grown close together in beds and borders. For example, plant marigolds with tomatoes to deter aphids, sow mustard seeds around brassicas to prevent flea beetle damage, while garlic planted around roses can deter aphids. You can also interplant rows of carrots with onions or leeks to disguise the smell that attracts carrot fly.

56 HELP THROUGH THE WINTER

Create overwintering homes for ladybirds (ladybugs) and lacewings, which are particularly voracious aphid-eaters but sensitive to cold winters. Bundle short sections of hollow bamboo canes together and place in a sheltered spot.

57 MAKE YOUR OWN CLOCHES

Use old plastic water bottles to make cloches to protect young seedlings and plants from attack. Cut off the bottom, or cut in half, and remove the cap to allow air and water in. Place over your seedling and bury it into the soil for support.

58 DETER THE NIBBLERS

If rabbits and deer are a problem then try planting some of the following: azaleas, bamboos, buddleia, box, choisya, clematis, pampas grass, daphnes, euphorbias, gaultherias, hydrangeas, hypericums, peonies, rhododendrons, yew or vinca. In tough winters, though, even these may come under attack.

59 SCARY SCARECROW

Stuff some old clothes with newspaper, or for a longer-lasting solution, sew some hessian together. Fill with straw and use a broom handle for support. Old clothes, a hat and scarf provide the finishing touches to your scarecrow, and children will love creating his face. Hammer the broom handle into the ground and the birds will keep their distance.

60 USE YOUR OLD CDS

Put those unwanted CDs to good use by hanging them over your plants or newly laid lawn to scare away the birds. String them up on a length of twine supported by bamboo canes.

61 **CONSERVE WATER**

Hosepipes can suck up 1,000 litres (265 gallons) of water an hour and a sprinkler may use as much water in an hour as a family of four uses in a day. If you must have a hosepipe, then fit a trigger nozzle to control the flow. An aerating nozzle allows you to water roots without washing away the soil or having to use the less-efficient spray pattern.

62 **SAVE THE RAIN**

Divert water from your gutters into a water butt, or several if your roof area is large. Even in dry areas 24,000 litres (6,340 gallons) can be collected from the average roof. Make sure the butt is made from recycled plastic, position it close to your garden and look out for inexpensive butts offered by water companies.

63

GO GREY

Grey water is water that you've used, such as bathwater and washing-up water. It can be recycled to water your garden – either save the water yourself or install a special system of outlet pipes. But never store grey water, and don't use water that contains strong cleaning agents or chemicals. Don't use it on edible plants either.

64

INVEST IN DRIP IRRIGATION

A drip irrigation system uses a network of plastic pipes to carry a slow, even flow of low-pressure water to plants. It delivers water to the roots of plants and reduces water use by half. You can buy kits online or pay for expert installation.

65 BEAR DROUGHTS IN MIND

There are many drought-tolerant plants that will do well despite the summer heat – herbs of Mediterranean origin, for example. As a general rule, most plants with small, leathery and grasslike or succulent leaves will fare well in droughts, as will those with grey or hairy leaves.

66 YOUR TRUE WATER NEEDS

Your garden probably doesn't need as much water as you might think it does. A good soak every couple of weeks is better for plant growth than regular light watering, where the water never reaches the plant roots. Dig a hole of a spade's depth in your soil to test – only water if the soil feels dry to the touch.

CLEVER WATERING

67

Create a saucer-shaped dip in the soil around your plants to collect water and do your watering when it is cool – early morning or evening – to prevent the water evaporating.

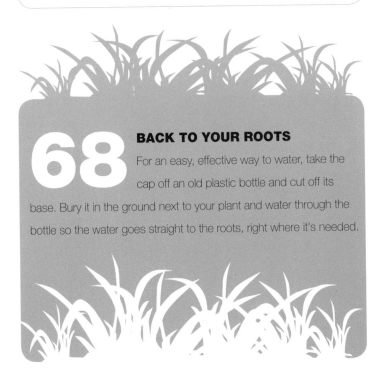

BACK TO YOUR ROOTS

68

For an easy, effective way to water, take the cap off an old plastic bottle and cut off its base. Bury it in the ground next to your plant and water through the bottle so the water goes straight to the roots, right where it's needed.

69 HELP OUT YOUR SOIL

Add compost to free-draining soils to improve water retention. For heavy soils, add compost and sharp sand or grit to open up the structure, improve water retention and reduce the chances of clay soils cracking during a dry summer.

70 ADJUST YOUR EXPECTATIONS

You may need to put your idea of lush, verdant lawn to the back of your mind and get used to some browning in the summer months. Your grass will soon recover in the autumn but you can help it by reducing the number of mowings and raising the cutting level of your mower.

71 PROVIDE SHELTER

Shade and shelter will stop the sun and wind drying out your garden. Use trees and shrubs to provide shade for other plants. Remember also that features like large trees and house walls can shelter the soil from rain.

72 FILTER YOUR WATER

Grey water from baths, showers and so on can be filtered through a bucket of straw – fill a well-perforated bucket with straw and allow the water to flow through it. Or, for the more ambitious, you can have a reed-bed system installed, where bacteria on the roots of reeds breaks down waste in the water.

73 WEATHER-WISE

How many times have you watered the garden only to watch the rain come down an hour or two later? Make sure you don't waste water by checking the weather forecast before you start.

74 PICK YOUR PLANTS WISELY

To maximize your chances of having healthy beautiful plants that don't need treatment for pests and disease, make sure you pick the plants to suit the condition of your garden. Find out what type of soil you have – clay, sandy, silt, peat or chalk. Study the path of the sun around your garden and investigate the average rainfall for your area. It's usually easy to check what grows well by taking a look at your neighbours' gardens.

75 START WITH SEEDS

Buying established plants from a garden centre might give you quick results, but transporting these plants to and from the shop will increase your carbon footprint. Ordering via the internet will reduce it or, even better, try growing your own from seed and discover just how satisfying it is.

76 LOOK FOR TRADITIONAL PLANT VARIETIES

The best seeds to choose are open pollinated, locally adapted, traditional seeds – preferably organic. Avoid the first-generation hybrids (F1 hybrids) available from mainstream suppliers as these reduce genetic diversity and often require fertilizers and pesticides to see the best results. There are 10,000 heritage apple varieties compared to just a few F1 hybrid apple types.

77

BUY ORGANIC SEEDS

Conventional seeds may well have been harvested from chemically grown plants and many are also treated with insecticides or fungicides prior to sale. Opt for organically certified seeds where available.

78

AVOID GM WHENEVER POSSIBLE

Genetically modified seeds – where the DNA of the plant has been changed – threaten the purity of seeds everywhere through cross-contamination. In some countries, such as the US, there is no legal requirement to label GM seeds, so the best way to avoid them is to buy organically certified seeds.

79

KEEP IT SIMPLE

Begin with the easier vegetable seeds: beans, lettuce, peas and peppers give the best chances of success because they produce seed the same season as they are planted. They are also mostly self-pollinating, which minimizes the need to be mindful of preventing cross-pollination.

80

SOW THE SEEDS OF SUCCESS

Make sure seeds are thoroughly dry before storing them. Keep them in paper envelopes or packets (not in plastic) in a cool, dry room – and never in a greenhouse. And don't forget to label them!

GET SWAPPING

81

Look out for local seed-swapping events – often held by allotment or gardening groups. Or search online for seed-saving or heritage seed organizations in your area that also provide advice on seed-saving techniques.

PROPAGATE ALL YOU CAN

82

Another way to avoid expensive, energy-guzzling trips to the garden centre is to propagate plants from existing plants – either yours or your friends' (but not annuals and biennials, which are always grown from seed). This will require some research on the best technique for the plant in question: division, stem cutting or layering.

83 SAVE NATIVE PLANTS

Wild plants are under threat from introduced invasive species, habitat loss and climate change. Do your bit by planting native wild plants in your garden. They will be better adapted to the local environment and repay you by requiring less maintenance. In the UK you can find native plants for your area using the Postcode Plants Database (www.nhm.ac.uk/fff). In the US, visit www.michbotclub.org/links/native_plant_society.htm to find the native plant society for your state.

84 WHERE DOES IT COME FROM?

Knowing the origins of a plant is especially important for native, wild plants and bulbs since many, such as bluebells and snowdrops in the UK and the small whorled pogonia and white lady's slipper in the US, are stolen from the wild.

85

BE A HERO

The only time it is acceptable to take plants from the wild is when they are about to be destroyed by development. If you pass a building site with wild plants that need saving, ask the land owner if you can take them.

86

BECOME A SAVVY CONSUMER

When buying plants, buy them in the smallest possible container as they are usually not much further behind in growing terms than those sold in larger, more expensive sizes. You can keep the pots for potting your own seedlings. Check also that the growing media in the pots does not contain peat (see tip 21).

87 RECYCLE PLASTIC INTO POTS

There are plenty of containers in which you can grow seedlings rather than throwing them away. Try yogurt and sour cream pots or polystyrene drinking cups, for example – just make sure water can drain out the bottom by piercing a few small holes in them first.

88 MAKE YOUR OWN

You can create seed pots out of egg boxes, toilet paper tubes – good for sweet peas that need room for long roots – and newspaper (search the internet for various sites that give folding instructions). Pots made from recycled paper and cardboard can be put straight into the ground without disturbing the seedlings' roots, as the pots will naturally biodegrade.

89

DON'T CREATE A CHEMICAL LAWN

The Pesticide Action Network North America claims that of the 30 commonly used lawn pesticides in the US, 19 are carcinogens, 13 linked with birth defects, 21 with reproductive effects, 15 with neurotoxicity, 26 with liver or kidney damage. Also, 27 are irritants and 11 can disrupt the hormone system. Do you want *your* kids to play in this kind of environment?

90

LEAVE THE LEAVES

Use your lawn mower to mow over leaves on the lawn with the grass box off – the shredded leaves will soon disappear into the lawn. Or keep the grass box on and add the chopped-up mown leaves and grass to a leaf-mould heap. They will rot more quickly than whole leaves.

91 DITCH THE PETROL (GAS) MOWER

The average lawnmower contributes about 1.2 kg (2 lb 10 oz) of CO_2 emissions a week and petrol mowers produce more CO_2 than electric versions. In fact, with 54 million Americans mowing their lawns each weekend with petrol-powered mowers, the mowers are said to account for at least 5% of America's air pollution.

92 USE YOUR OWN POWER

Other than ultra low-emission lawnmowers that can cut emissions by up to 80% over traditional models and improve fuel consumption, the best environmental option is to use manpower – so buy a push mower.

93 HARNESS THE SUN'S POWER

If your lawn – and budget – are big, consider a Swedish-built solar-powered 'auto mower', which has collision sensors to prevent it from clattering into your wall or patio.

94 REDUCE YOUR LAWN

If the size of your lawn means a push mower is impractical, then consider reducing the area you have to cut by creating wildflower meadows and areas of longer grass. Both are great for wildlife.

95 CUT BACK ON CUTTING

Reduce the number of times you cut the grass. This will save energy and benefit the lawn in dry climates, as longer grass shades the soil and also traps dew.

96 PLANT A HERB OR FRAGRANT LAWN

Add to the biodiversity of your garden by planting low-growing aromatic herbs and flowers in your lawn. A chamomile lawn can be very drought-resistant and is fragrant when walked on or cut. Other plants to try include wild thyme, yarrow, Corsican mint and white clover.

97 TURF REINFORCEMENT

Rubber crumb, which is made from recycled car tyres, can be sprinkled over your lawn and brushed in. It will eventually be drawn down where it will create a more open soil structure and improve the root structure of your lawn.

98 USE A MULCHING MOWER

A mulching mower recycles grass clippings by chopping them into fine particles before pushing the particles down into the turf where they provide moisture and nutrients for your lawn. This, in turn, reduces the need for any fertilizers. A season's worth of mulching is said to provide 25% of a lawn's fertilizer requirements.

99

KEEP YOUR CUTTINGS

Either let your grass cuttings stay on the grass to slowly release nutrients back into the soil or use them as a mulch for other plants in the garden – mix with leaves and spread them around shrubs in the autumn.

100

MOLE CONTROL

If moles are making a mess of your garden, try using a solar-powered mole deterrent. This is a plastic stake that emits a sonic pulse into the ground to discourage moles from tunnelling under your lawn.

STAY ON TOP OF YOUR LAWN

Rather than relying on a battery of synthetic fertilizers that can contaminate ground water, ensure your lawn is in top condition in the first place. Top-dress it with leaf mould and compost in autumn and apply an organically certified fertilizer if absolutely necessary.

GIVE BULBS A GO

Break up the monotony of a lawn and attract insects to your garden with drifts of spring flowers such as crocus, snowdrops, snake's head fritillaries and dwarf narcissis. These bulbs can be planted under the turf and will grow well if the lawn is given a trim in late autumn.

103 TEA-BAG LAWN

Fill gaps in your lawn by reusing your tea bags. Simply place moist, used tea bags on a bare spot, then sprinkle it with grass seed. The tea bag will provide moisture as it gradually decomposes.

104 GO NATIVE

Native plants are better suited to meet the needs of local wildlife, and some wildlife species are entirely dependent on the availability of certain native plants. The Karner Blue butterfly in the US, for example, is endangered because of the disappearance of its larval host plant, wild lupine. In the UK, all native butterfly species are suffering from loss of habitat and in the past 200 years, five species have become extinct.

105 KEEP IT MESSY

The more quiet, undisturbed places in your garden the better it is for wildlife. Leave drifts of autumn leaves under hedges – you might find a hibernating hedgehog below them. Don't remove woody stems from pampas grass in the winter as they make excellent nest sites for solitary bees, while slow worms will thank you for rough grass, rocks and logs, and ladybirds (ladybugs) enjoy sheltering in hollow-stemmed plants left through winter.

106 LEARN TO LOVE BATS

A tiny common pipistrelle can eat around 3,000 midges, mosquitoes and other small flies in a single night. Moths, beetles and crane flies (daddy long legs) are popular with other species. Encourage bats into your garden by planting a mixture of flowering plants, trees and shrubs to attract a diversity of insects, especially night-blossoming versions. Bats are a protected species in many countries.

107 MAKE A LACEWING MOTEL

Cut the base off a 2 litre (4.2 pint) empty soft drink bottle. Slide a roll of corrugated cardboard inside the bottle and string some fine wire across the bottom to keep it from falling out. Tie string around the top of the bottle, with the cap left on, and hang in a sheltered position by the end of summer. The lacewing larvae will thank you by eating your aphids.

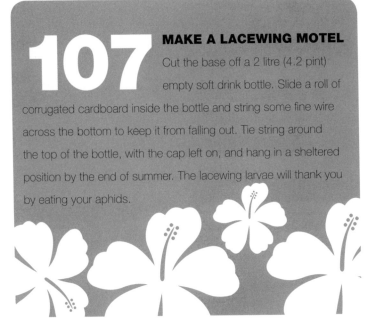

108 COMPOST WITH CARE

Compost heaps can shelter slow worms and toads, and grass snakes that may also lay their eggs there. Take extra care when turning your heap or digging out the compost.

109

FEED THE BIRDS

Plant food for birds in your garden. Grow sunflowers and leave the seed heads on or string them up for birds to feed on. Leave rosehips on the roses to go to seed over winter – again, the birds will make good use of them.

110

LEAVE OLD TREE STUMPS

Aged tree stumps are an important habitat for many insects, especially the endangered stag beetle, and a rotten log by a pond provides a great site for egg-laying dragonflies.

111 FEATHER A NEST

Keep fur that you have groomed from your cat or dog (and any hair from home haircuts) and put it out on a bird table or high on a twiggy bush in spring – it could be just what a nesting bird is looking for.

112 SHARE YOUR FRUIT WITH THE BIRDS

If you leave some fruit on your bushes, trees and vines you will be helping birds and other wildlife. Not only does the fruit provide a valuable source of food for animals but the trees also allow shelter for insects, birds and small mammals.

113

MAKE YOUR OWN BIRD FEEDER

Stick two twigs through the bottom third of a small plastic water bottle so that they cross over each other and leave enough of the twigs sticking out for the birds to stand on. Half fill with bird food – nuts and seeds – and hang it on a nearby tree using string pushed through the top third.

114

LURE IN INSECTS

If you have a variety of insects in your garden you are likely to attract plenty of wildlife, such as bats, to feast on them, so tempt them in with a mix of flowers. Try flowers with long narrow petal tubes, such as evening primrose and honeysuckle for moths, pale flowers that can be seen in poor light to attract insects at dusk, and single flowers, which tend to produce more nectar than double varieties; also flowers with insect-friendly landing platforms and short florets, such as those in the daisy or carrot families.

115 PLANT CLIMBERS

Climbing plants, such as ivy and wild honeysuckle, will provide cover for nesting birds, hibernation sites for butterflies and food for insects. So get busy putting up that trellis!

116 A FEW HOLES WON'T HURT

Don't fill in holes in walls and fencing, especially screw holes, as these can be used by leafcutter and red mason bees – both are docile and won't cause additional damage. They are two of the best pollinators.

117 BUILD A POND

A pond is an absolute essential for any self-respecting wildlife gardener, but make sure it has gently sloping edges to make it easy for hedgehogs and frogs to get out – it's not uncommon to find hedgehogs drowned in garden ponds.

118 MORE FISH, LESS FROGS

Fish eat frogspawn and tadpoles so if you want frogs in abundance to keep your insect levels down, you may want to limit the number of fish in your pond.

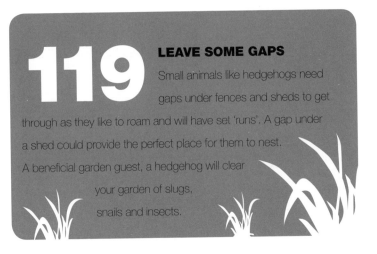

119 LEAVE SOME GAPS

Small animals like hedgehogs need gaps under fences and sheds to get through as they like to roam and will have set 'runs'. A gap under a shed could provide the perfect place for them to nest. A beneficial garden guest, a hedgehog will clear your garden of slugs, snails and insects.

120 FATTEN THEM UP

Birds benefit from fat as valuable food source, especially during the winter, so make sure you provide fat feeders in your garden. You can make your own by mixing solid fat such as lard or dripping with seed, nuts, raisins and bird peanuts. Push into drilled holes in small logs or branches, or try an upside-down coconut or yogurt pot.

121

CREATE A WILDFLOWER MEADOW

To make your own meadow, you can leave an area of grass uncut and see what grows (although you should cut it at some point to stop shrubby plants taking over). Or sow wildflowers in an area of cleared ground – ideally of poor quality soil to keep the weeds at bay. Wildflower seed mixes are readily available.

122

OFFER SHELTER TO BEES

Bees, especially orchard mason bees, will make their homes in drilled blocks of wood (drill holes into a piece of soft wood). You can also use paper drinking straws stacked on their sides in a waterproof box. Search the internet for ways to make bee homes or try: www.fs.fed.us/wildflowers/pollinators/beebox.

123 **KEEP CATS AWAY**

You don't want to fatten the birds up only to find you're making a tasty meal for the local cats! Make sure you put your bird table at least 2 m (6 ft 6 in) from undergrowth that might provide sneaky hiding spaces for cats, and keep nesting boxes well out of their way. Also, add a bell to your cat's collar as a warning to birds.

124 **DON'T FEED WILD ANIMALS**

As a general rule, apart from birds, wild animals should not be fed. The food you give them could affect their health and becoming reliant on humans for food could limit an animal's survival skills. Remember to properly dispose of food remains and packaging.

125 GROW YOUR OWN

Reduce your carbon footprint, save money, amaze your children and experience the true meaning of pride by growing your own fruit, vegetables and herbs. You don't need a huge amount of space, a greenhouse or lots of special equipment to be eating a 'house' salad in summer and homemade soup in winter.

126 ROTATE YOUR CROPS

To help control pests and diseases and improve the fertility of your soil, make sure you don't grow the same vegetables in the same place each year. The four plant groups to rotate are: roots, cereals, brassicas and legumes – check which group yours belong in and move them round each year.

127 START SIMPLE

Be sure to keep your enthusiasm high by starting with some easy vegetables and fruits. For a big harvest with minimal effort try tomatoes and courgettes (zucchini). Strawberries are a firm favourite and some herbs and lettuces should thrive on your windowsill, where you hopefully won't forget to water them!

128 USE NATURAL TIES

When tying up climbing plants choose ties made of natural fibre or buy a roll of jute string that will eventually rot, rather than plastic coated wires. The latter might also damage your plants by cutting into them.

129 MUSHROOM MAKER

You can purchase hardwood logs that are already colonized with mushrooms to grow in your garden or even buy mushroom spawn which can be grown on toilet paper rolls. Always buy logs from a sustainable source.

130 CUT BACK ON CUT FLOWERS

In the UK, 80% of bought cut flowers are imported, usually by air, and in the US imports make up about two-thirds of the cut-flower market. Reduce your carbon footprint by growing your own supply. You'll need a sunny spot with well-drained, fertile soil and some shelter from strong winds. Varieties to try include: dahlias, chrysanthemums, zinnias, snapdragons, cosmos and sweet william. Be sure to pick regularly to encourage more blooms and to prevent flowers from trying to set seed.

131 BOOST YOUR CULINARY OPTIONS

As well as fruit and vegetables, be sure to grow some herbs, if only on a windowsill. Start with those you use regularly and experience the thrill of snipping minutes before eating. This will also save you buying costly vacuum-packed, pesticide-laden herbs that have been flown in to a supermarket near you. Try chives, mint, basil and parsley.

132 EXPERIENCE NATURAL FRAGRANCE

Instead of relying on toxic synthetic fragrances, grow fragrant flowers and herbs which, fresh or dried, will fill your home with natural scents. To make a simple pot-pourri, mix together dried rose petals, lavender flowers and leaves, lemon balm leaves and marigold petals in equal amounts. A few drops of essential oil will revive the scent when it starts to fade.

133

A PLANT-BASED MEDICINE CHEST

Grow herbs that are known for their medicinal properties and create your own remedies. Among those worth trying are: coriander or cilantro (chewing the leaves or infusing as a tea is said to relieve an upset stomach); calendula (steep the flowers in hot water and use the drained liquid as a healing mouthwash for gums); and thyme (as a tea sweetened with honey it can help relieve sore throats and coughs).

134

HERBAL PEST CONTROL

Instead of sprinkling poisons around your home to kill pest invasions, you can use herbs from your garden. Try hanging sprigs of fresh sage, pennyroyal, rue or tansy in your kitchen cupboards to deter ants. Both ants and flies are repelled by the smell of mint so plant some by your kitchen door and windows. Dried bay leaves placed in flour, rice and pulses keeps weevils away, too.

135 PLANT-BASED CLEANING

Simmer the leaves and flowering stems of rosemary, eucalyptus, juniper, lavender, sage or thyme in water for 30 minutes. Strain the water and use as a disinfectant around the home. Refrigerated, it will last for up to a week.

136 KEEP YOUR TREES

Trees are good for you, the climate and wildlife. Patients have been shown to recover from surgery more quickly when their hospital room had a view of trees. Trees provide a safe home for many species of birds and insects; they also filter the air, provide shade and absorb carbon dioxide.

137 THE RIGHT TREE IN THE RIGHT PLACE

When choosing a tree, be sure you will still be happy with the position of a tree once it has reached maturity. You don't necessarily have to keep it far from your house. Tree roots do not have the capacity to break up the large concrete foundation block of a modern building, but houses built on shrinkable clay soil may be affected indirectly because roots can dry the soil – and lead to subsidence – but this can become worse if a tree is suddenly removed.

138 BEING SMALL IS NO EXCUSE

There is a tree for every garden! Even in a small garden there is usually room to plant at least one tree. Smaller species include acers, Tibetan cherry, crab apple, pussy willow and hazel.

139

WILDLIFE-FRIENDLY SPECIES

Willow, birch and beech are favoured by many native insects. Ermine moth larvae feed on the leaves of the bird cherry tree. Yew and holly with their dense foliage and branches, are good for greenfinches and treecreepers often nest behind the loose bark of larger mature trees. Bats feed on caterpillars that live on willow trees.

140

GO EASY ON THE PRUNING

If you're pruning a tree, do it in the autumn when there aren't any birds nesting. Try to leave some hollow tree branches (as long as they're not threatening to fall off), since these provide good nesting places for tawny owls and other birds.

141

USE YOUR TRIMMINGS

Don't just throw out the twigs and branches cut from your tree or hedge. Some will make stakes to support climbing plants – coppiced hazel is particularly good for supporting peas, while others can be used to make trellis, edging for beds, or woven baskets and screens.

142

PLANT A HEDGE

Hedges are living fences which are great for wildlife – hedgerows have been recorded as providing shelter or food for 600 plant species, 1,500 insects, 65 birds and 20 mammals. They also make better windbreaks than fences since they absorb the wind and can be a stronger barrier against intruders, particularly those comprised of prickly hawthorn, blackthorn and holly. You'll also be helping to replace the many hedges lost to intensive farming – it is estimated that 5% of UK hedgerows are lost each year due to neglect or removal.

143

MAKE YOUR HEDGEROW MIXED

Hedges provide a natural habitat for many insects, birds and mammals, as well as security, privacy and shelter. The best hedges for wildlife contain several species that come into leaf, flower and fruit at different times. Try hawthorn, blackthorn, guelder rose, field maple (hedge maple), yew, beech, native privet, berberis and holly. You can also include small trees, such as crab apple and elder.

144

AVOID LEYLANDII

A Leylandii cypress hedge may grow quickly – 1 m (3 ft) per year up to a height of 45 m (150 ft) – and does provide nesting opportunities for birds, but the trees suck up large amounts of water and nutrients from the soil, cast deep shade and are of less benefit for wildlife than traditional hedges grown with native species.

145 TRIM BY HAND

There's no need for power-consuming electric hedge trimmers. Use long-handled secateurs or get out your ladder and use pruning shears.

146 NEW-STONE ALTERNATIVES

New stone comes at a high environmental cost due to the energy used in quarrying and transporting it. Alternatives include using reclaimed stone or building cob walls – local mud mixed with straw or heather, rammed earth walls, wattle and daub or a hazel lattice covered in mud and straw.

147

WAYS WITH WILLOW

Willow is very tough and fast-growing. It can be woven into a living screen to make domes, arbours and screens that will then shoot and grow into a larger growing structures. Or you can create a soil-filled framework of dry willow in which ground cover plants are grown. Willow screens make good windbreaks.

148

A GREEN SCREEN

There are a few green-screening products on the market. One consists of a welded wire trellising system available as a standalone fence; it is filled with earth and plants grow over it. The other is made from recycled plastic tubing covered in coir fibre, a natural waste product, which is designed to be covered with climbing plants.

149 A SUNFLOWER SCREEN

Sunflowers can make an unusual summer screen. Choose several varieties that grow to different heights. Sow seeds outdoors in April and by mid-summer you will have a flowering screen and an abundant source of cut flowers.

150 GROW YOUR OWN BAMBOO

Instead of using bamboo that has been flown across the globe, grow your own for use as plant supports or screens. It takes three years to grow sufficiently to make 2–3 m (6–9 ft) long canes. Cut above a joint, dry them slowly for up to six months and lash together to form a screen.

151

HEAD UPWARDS

Train climbing plants up fences and walls. They provide sheltering sites for insects and spiders, nesting and roosting spots for birds, and beautiful flowers as a bonus. Climbers that are best for wildlife include honeysuckle, ivy, wild clematis, wisteria and Virginia creeper.

152

BUILD YOUR OWN TRELLIS

Help your climbers on their way up by building a trellis from hazel poles. Cut two poles to about 2 m (6 ft 6 in) long and drill a hole at each end approximately 50 cm (20 in) from the mid-point. Attach two lengths of sisal rope to the wall or fence, 1.5 m (5 ft) apart, and thread the hazel poles onto the rope, tying a knot in both lengths of rope after each one. To finish off, tie a knot under the final rod and trim away the excess.

153

BRING YOUR WALLS ALIVE

Seek expert advice on turning the walls around your garden or your home into 'living walls' – a vertical garden where plants are rooted in a fibrous material that is then anchored to a wall. They can provide the same insulating benefits as green roofs, give e a home to wildlife and reduce the possibility of flooding.

154

WHERE DOES YOUR FENCING COME FROM?

The wood used in your fencing could well have come from forests that are not managed sustainably – Illegal logging is rife in Russia, for example, where the larch for many timber fences is sourced. It is also likely to have been treated with toxic chemical preservatives. Instead, always use untreated wood from a sustainably managed forest that carries the Forest Stewardship Council (FSC) label.

155 USE NATURAL RESISTANCE

Some woods are better able to resist decay. For example, oak and sweet chestnut will last 20 years when in contact with the soil and 40 years above ground, while larch lasts ten years in soil and 20 years above it.

156 EXPLORE SYNTHETIC WOOD OPTIONS

There are a range of synthetic wood products now available made from recycled plastic and polystyrene, such as waste packaging for electronic goods and waste drinking cups. They generate no waste during manufacture and are completely recyclable. What's more, they are maintenance-free and can be used in fencing or elsewhere in your garden. Just double check the amount of recycled material used before you buy.

157 USE AN ORGANIC PRESERVATIVE

There is an alternative to toxic, synthetic preservatives. For fence panels that are not in contact with the soil, apply  linseed oil or similar products that allow the wood to breathe. Boron-based timber preservatives are also acceptable in organic gardening since they are safe for people and the environment.

158 BEWARE RAILWAY SLEEPERS

Popular though they may be for edging raised borders, old railway sleepers have often been treated with coal tar creosote, which the Environmental Protection Agency (EPA) in the US has determined is a probable human carcinogen, and is banned from use in the European Union. The creosote can seep out in hot weather. It doesn't mean you have to give up these recycled products altogether but do make sure they are not used where they will come into contact with children and food, and don't use them where there is a risk of frequent skin contact. Better still, track down untreated sleepers.

159

MAKE GOOD USE OF YOUR ROOF

Installing a green roof on top of your garden shed will help provide a home for wildlife and reduce the potential for flooding as a green roof lowers water run-off from a roof by at least 50%. It will also protect your roof from the effects of the weather and ultra-violet light, and will help keep a potting shed cool during the hot summer months.

160

KEEP PATIOS SMALLER

Paved areas absorb more heat than green spaces and release this heat back into the atmosphere in the cool of the night. This can significantly contribute to temperatures rising in heavily paved urban areas – called the 'heat island effect' – which in turn leads to greater use of energy-hungry air conditioners. Keep as much of your garden as green as you can.

161 NOTHING IS CONCRETE

After water, concrete is the second most-used product on the planet, but a key ingredient of it is cement, the manufacture of which produces more than 5% of global carbon dioxide emissions. If you must use concrete source a mix that uses recycled aggregates and which replaces Portland cement with materials that would otherwise be landfilled, such as PFA (pulverized fuel ash) or GGBS (ground granulated blastfurnace slag).

162 REUSE AN OLD PATIO

If you are getting rid of a paved area in your garden, be sure to reuse as much of it as possible. Broken paving can be placed at the bottom of pots to assist with drainage. It can also be crushed and used in drainage systems, and unwanted rubble may be used to build a stone-and-earth mound – great for hibernating newts, frogs and lizards.

163 WHAT LIES BENEATH

Paving is often laid on concrete, sand and crushed rock but these elements are all non-renewable, so ensure you use only the minimum depth necessary. Where safe, lay stone without mortar or concrete to allow for future reuse; re-source old gravels and sand from beneath paving you have demolished; and use recycled brick or concrete instead of new quarried material.

164 BREAK UP THE SEA OF PAVING

A terrace doesn't have to consist of a big strip of paving. Plant low-growing herbs in cracks between paving slabs – fill with compost and sow seed in spring. Keep watered and avoid treading on them until established. Varieties to try include lady's mantle, Corsican mint and creeping thymes.

165

BEWARE TOXIC DECKS

A lot of decking is treated with toxic preservatives and in the not-too-distant past is likely to have been pressure-treated with chromated copper arsenate (CCA), which is 22% pure arsenic. CCA-treated wood for residential use is being phased out, but supplies might still exist in stores, so ask before you buy.

166

GO TO THE RECLAMATION YARD

Salvaged timber is a great option for decking, provided it has not been treated with preservatives. Look for a durable hardwood, such as oak, which does not need a preservative. If you can't find used timber then make sure the timber you buy carries the Forest Stewardship Council (FSC) label, which means it will have come from a sustainably managed forest.

167 TRY ALTERNATIVE DECKS

There are a variety of eco-friendly decking options out there, such as tiles which snap together made from the durable Bolivian Ipe hardwood. This is naturally resistant to rot, decay, insects and mould without chemical treatment.

168 WALK WITH RUBBER

Try walking on rubber when outdoors by laying floor tiles made of 100% recycled rubber designed for use outside the home. They're anti-slip and weatherproof, and even come in a variety of colours!

169 GREEN CLEAN YOUR DECK

Decks are notorious for getting slippery and slimy after a year or so in a damp climate, but rather than use harsh chemicals to clean them, look instead for green alternatives that are non-toxic and biodegradable.

170 USE A BRUSH

There's no need to powerwash your decking with a hose. Save water by giving it a good brush with a firm-bristled broom during dry weather.

171 GO WITH GRASS PAVERS

You don't have to pave over an area of your lawn to make a pathway or drive; instead install a grass paver, a grass-reinforcement system which consists of a hollow grid (ideally made from recycled plastic) that is filled with topsoil and seeded with grass. These prevent erosion of the soil and absorb storm water, preventing it from flowing straight into the drains.

172 STONE AT A PRICE

Imports of natural stone account for around 10% of the UK market for home paving, but sandstone from India is being mined often by very young children, working long hours in inhumane conditions. Many stone quarries in China are no better. Seek a supplier who can prove its stone is ethically sourced or find your stone at a reclamation yard.

173 ADOPT SUDS

A Sustainable Urban Drainage System (SUDS) will prevent flash flooding that is likely with more intense periods of rain expected as a result of climate change. Paving, tarmac and concrete increase the amount of rainwater that runs off by as much as 5%, so avoid creating heavily paved areas – set paving in sand, rather than mortar, use resin-bonded gravel and aggregates held in cells made from recycled plastic, or use permeable paving with gaps that allow water to drain into the soil or to be stored.

174 USE RE-USE

If you do choose conventional concrete block and slab paving, bricks or cobbles, try re-use. Ask at salvage yards, municipal waste recovery centres and check out freecycle sites online. When laying paving, slope it so that the water runs onto the garden.

175 NOT-SO-FRIENDLY GRAVEL

Gravel is often recommended as an environmentally friendly material because it allows water to drain freely into the soil and consumes no energy in manufacture, but it might have been strip-mined off the seabed, destroying marine life, or removed from existing river systems. Ask your supplier to confirm that habitats at source are not threatened by the removal of the gravel.

176 STEPPING STONES

Ask yourself whether you really need a whole path – it would be far better to use just a few stepping stones or set old logs into the grass than to add to the amount of concrete or stone already in your garden. You could also create paths from chipped wood or bark, recycled glass chips, crushed brick or recycled aggregates.

177 LIMIT YOUR LIMESTONE

Demand for limestone pavement stone for use in garden rockeries is leading to the devastation of naturally occurring limestone pavements and the special plants that live in them. There is no way of telling whether water-worn limestone is from a legal or illegal source, and large amounts of illegally obtained pavement stone are being sold. Wherever possible use reclaimed stone or buy moulded resin rocks cast to look like pieces of limestone pavement.

178 BUILD ALTERNATIVE RAISED BEDS

There are plenty of eco-friendly raised bed options. Use old bits of wood or concrete available from salvage yards or local refuse centres; create them from old tyres stacked together. Or use railway sleepers, but check they are untreated if you are growing edibles. You can also buy recycled raised bed kits made from recycled milk jugs and plastic scrap.

179

TOO HOT TO HANDLE

Over 600,000 gas-powered heaters adorn the patios and decking areas of UK households alone, adding in excess of 350,000 tonnes of additional carbon emissions to the atmosphere every year. Their use has also exploded in hotels and bars since the smoking ban came into effect. Our advice? Just put on another sweater!

180

NO NEED FOR NEW

With eBay and various other websites offering the opportunity to buy or swap unwanted items, you should be able to find garden furniture to your liking at a fraction of the cost of buying new. Try to avoid driving miles to pick it up, though.

181 SAY NO TO TROPICAL HARDWOODS

Avoid garden furniture made from tropical hardwoods which comes from uncertified sources – the UK is the main importer of tropical hardwood furniture in Europe. Instead, look out for alternatives, such as furniture made from recycled aluminium, a garden bench created from reclaimed scaffold boards, tables made from cable drums and recycled timber, loungers constructed from reclaimed teak and recycled-tyre stools.

182 MAKE YOUR OWN FURNITURE

If you live in the country then it shouldn't be too hard to find tree stumps to make into tables or seats, or you could go to a local sawmill and ask for off-cuts. Ensure the stump is set into the ground and then shape using a chainsaw. Temporary furniture can also be made by roping together straw bales.

183 ORGANIC FAIR-TRADE HAMMOCKS

A hammock is one of the simplest and best seating options out there but look out for hammocks made from organic cotton that carry a fair-trade mark to guarantee good pay and working conditions for those making them. Make sure also that you use trees to support the hammock rather than buying a metal or wood stand. If forced to purchase a stand, buy a wooden one and check it carries the Forest Stewardship Council (FSC) mark.

184 SWING INTO ACTION

You don't have to buy play equipment for the kids to keep them active. If you have a tree with a strong branch, make your own swing by tying a recycled tyre to the branch or drill a hole through the centre of a disc of wood (an old chopping board would do). Insert some strong rope through the hole and knot it. Secure it really well to the tree by looping over the branch and knotting firmly. Test it before letting the kids play on it.

185 BEWARE OLD PLAY EQUIPMENT

Until relatively recently most wood for outdoor use, including play equipment, was pressure treated with chromated copper arsenate (CCA). Since 2004, in the US, and later in the EU, CCA has not been allowed for use in woods destined for residential uses due to health concerns over the arsenic used, which is a known carcinogen. But if you buy second-hand play equipment it might have been treated with CCA – check whether the wood has a greenish tint.

186 SOLAR-POWERED WATER FEATURES

Imagine sitting on your patio, sipping your drink, while listening to the sound of water splashing. This tranquil moment is easy to create with the purchase of a solar-powered water feature – you can even buy a bird bath complete with detachable solar-powered fountain.

187

ADD A 'GREEN' FOUNTAIN

Reduce the amount of electricity used in your garden by installing a solar-powered fountain in your pond, which can be lit with floating solar lights. As well as looking good, a fountain will also oxygenate the water and can circulate up to 380 litres (100 gallons) per hour. You can also purchase solar-powered pond oxygenators for this purpose.

188

PUT A BALL IN IT

Instead of installing a pond heater, just leave a tennis ball floating on the surface of your pond in winter. You can remove it on frosty mornings to ensure the pond does not freeze over entirely. Avoid breaking the ice or pouring salt or hot water into the pond as this could be damaging to fish and anything else living in there.

189

REDUCE THE NEED FOR MAINTENANCE

Site your pond where it receives maximum sunlight and minimum leaf litter. If leaves still blow into it, put a net across the pond in autumn and add the collected leaves to your leaf mould pile. The better the quality of the water, the better it will be for wildlife.

190

MAKE THE MOST OF YOUR POND

Avoid non-native water plants and build your pond near longer grass or a border to give any wildlife that come to drink and bathe there cover. Position it near a wood pile or rockery for extra cover for hibernating newts and amphibians, or simply leave some loose stones and wood close to the edges of the pond.

191 CREATE A MINI-POND

You can use virtually any water-tight container to make a pond – old enamel sinks or stone troughs, for example. Whichever you choose, fill it with rainwater (if using tap water, allow to stand for a few days to allow the chlorine to evaporate) and plant with native plants.

192 WEED WITH CARE

Don't use chemicals to kill weeds such as blanket weed in your pond. Clear weeds by hand and leave for a while on the edge to allow any insects it contains to find their way back to the water. Then compost the remains. The best time to clear a pond is in the early autumn when it's least disruptive to wildlife.

193 LEARN TO LOVE THE DARK

Light pollution is a growing problem around the world. Not only is it a waste of energy, it also has a detrimental effect on birds and animals. Stray night-time light can confuse their natural patterns and affect breeding cycles. While the problem is mostly due to badly designed street and road lighting, security lights and floodlights, you can do your bit either by letting your garden get dark at night or using low-intensity lights that are directed downwards.

194 USE THE SUN'S POWER

There is a huge range of solar-powered outdoor lighting available now, so there's no excuse for running electric cables round your garden. Use just a few lights where you need them most, such as along paths or near terraces, but be sure to keep some areas of your garden as dark as possible for the sake of wildlife.

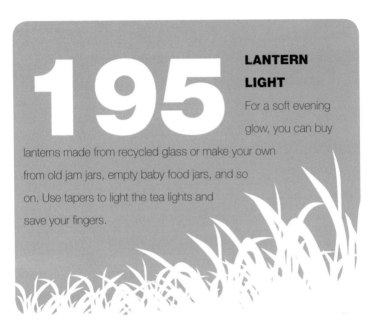

195 LANTERN LIGHT

For a soft evening glow, you can buy lanterns made from recycled glass or make your own from old jam jars, empty baby food jars, and so on. Use tapers to light the tea lights and save your fingers.

196 NATURAL INSECT REPELLENTS

An evening eating out under the stars on your patio can be ruined by mosquitoes. Try citronella oil – in candles or in a candle-lit vaporizer – to deter the little critters. Keep some tea tree oil handy to soothe any bites, too.

197 BE CAREFUL HOW YOU BAG IT

A lot of lugging things round goes on in a garden – prunings to the compost, harvested veg to the kitchen, leaves to your leafmould container. Instead of using plastic sacks to carry these items, look for eco-friendly alternatives such as long-lasting trugs made from recycled plastic or tyres, woven bags made of recycled plastic and biodegradable jute leaf and hessian sacks.

198 PICK GREEN FOR YOUR PICNIC

Make the most of your lawn or the shade of a tree by spreading a picnic rug out and eating al fresco. You can buy picnic blankets made from 'shoddy' wool, which is the wool left over from the production of virgin wool blankets, and biodegradeable picnic sets made from sustainable bamboo husk, which can be composted.

199

SAVE ON PLASTIC LABELS

Instead of buying plastic plant labels to mark where you have planted your seeds, consider investing in labels that you can re-use, such as hand-carved green oak labels. Or make your own by cutting strips from old margarine or ice-cream tubs. Children's wooden ice-lolly (popsicle) sticks are also worth saving for this purpose and they will biodegrade.

200

CONTAIN YOUR GARDEN

A great range of plants can be grown in containers on your windowsill, balcony or patio. There's almost nothing that won't grow in a container so try some of these: tumbler tomatoes, strawberries, trailing cucumber, oriental greens, chard, and herbs such as chives, parsley and mint.

201 MAKE YOUR OWN

There are plenty of objects that can be turned into plant pots – try old tyres, a chimney pot, ceramic bowls, an old wheelbarrow or even larger tin cans. Just make sure you drill some holes in the bottom to allow water to drain. If you want to age the ceramic containers, paint yogurt on the outside and keep in a shady spot to promote the growth of lichen.

202 USE WATER-RETAINING GRANULES

These will help to reduce the amount of water needed in your containers, many of which dry out far more quickly than in beds and borders. Manufacturers claim that an increase in soil water-holding capacity of 300–800% is possible in some soils.

203 NO NEED FOR MOSS

Sphagnum moss is commonly used as a liner for hanging baskets as it keeps plants moist, while allowing oxygen to reach them. However, this moss comes from peat bogs and its use threatens the already depleted precious environment (see tip 21). Use alternatives such as recycled wool (cut an old woolly sweater to fit), coir or hemp fibre.

204 COVER THE TOP

Containers are notorious for needing a lot of water because the growing media dries out quickly. To prevent some of this moisture loss, cover the surface of the soil with mulch, such as wood chippings or pebbles.

205

STAYING ALIVE

To keep your plants alive while you are on holiday (and spare the neighbours from having to constantly come round and water them for you), put a small plastic bottle filled with water (with one minute pinhole in its base which sweats rather than drips) on top of the soil in the pot. This will slowly drip water into the pot.

206

POTS CAN BE MOVED!

Instead of constantly watering your container-grown plants consider moving them to a shadier spot during a long hot, dry spell to prevent evaporation. Equally, move your hanging baskets to a cooler location if you are going to be away for more than a day or so.

207

LINE YOUR POT

Terracotta pots in particular tend to lose water quickly. When planting up a new pot, line it with a plastic carrier bag, with drainage holes pierced in the bottom, to prevent water loss from the sides.

208

USE A GUTTER

A piece of leftover plastic guttering can be used to grow salad leaves. Take 1 m (3 ft) lengths of guttering, fill with compost, sprinkle with a pinch of salad seeds and cover with a thin layer of compost. Keep on a windowsill and the salad should be ready to plant out into a bigger container or in your garden after three weeks or so, at which point you can start off your next lot of seedlings.

209 BE WARY OF BARBECUES

Just as with patio heaters which can release 7 kg (15 lb) of CO_2 in just a couple of hours, some of the latest top-of-the-range barbecue grills are among the least eco-friendly garden accessories, relying on gas or electricity to power them. You might as well stay in the kitchen! Keep it small and simple with a homemade barbecue, or buy a small one with a plain design that uses materials from a sustainable source.

210 MAKE YOUR OWN BRICK BBQ

You can build your own brick barbecue grill – a great way to use leftover or salvaged bricks – or use a roasting tin instead. It should be about 8 cm (3 in) deep and you can use a metal cake rack or some chicken wire as the grill. Stand it on some bricks but be absolutely certain it has cooled down before touching the tin. You'll find lots of ideas for brick barbecues on the internet.

211 AVOID BRIQUETTES

Half of all UK barbecues use wood charcoal, but up to 90% of the 40,000 tonnes of charcoal burnt in the UK each year is sourced from abroad, often from vulnerable tropical forests and mangrove swamps. There's enough woodland near most of us to be able to supply local charcoal, which also reduces transport pollution. Look for local, sustainable suppliers that carry the Forest Stewardship Council (FSC) logo.

212 CHARCOAL DANGERS

In the US, 63% of barbecues are fired with briquettes, which consist of waste timber and sawdust mixed with cornflour (cornstarch) to bind, and a hydrocarbon solvent, similar to lighter fluid, to help them start easily. But according to the US Environmental Protection Agency, charcoal briquettes release 105 times more carbon monoxide per unit of energy than propane and a lot of toxic volatile organic compounds. However, propane or liquid petroleum gas is not the answer either, as it's a fossil fuel and a net contributor to atmospheric CO_2 levels.

213 USE A CHIMNEY STARTER

Lighter fluid or self-lighting briquettes will give off volatile organic compounds (VOCs) when burnt, which in some people can cause irritation to the eyes, nose and throat, and sometimes more severe reactions. If you are using charcoal, try a chimney starter instead. This consists of a metal cylinder with a grate near the bottom – unlit charcoal is put inside the cylinder and newspaper is placed under the grate and lit. The charcoal at the bottom of the cylinder lights first and the 'chimney effect' ignites the remaining charcoal above.

214 ALL-NATURAL FIRELIGHTERS

It is now possible to buy natural firelighters online. Fair-trade fire sticks from Guatemala are handmade from the stump of the ocote tree. They are 80% resin but dry to the touch and make good natural firelighters.

215 SWEDISH HELPER

You'll wonder how you managed without Swedish FireSteels. Developed by the Swedish Defence Department, they produce a spark up to 3,000°C (5,432°F) in the wet or cold by moving a striker across the steel. Ideal for starting barbecues, provided you have some kindling to hand.

216 MAKE IT A RARE TREAT

You should be aware of the health risks associated with barbecues. Smoke from both charcoal and wood produces not only hydrocarbons but also tiny soot particles that pollute the air and can aggravate heart and lung problems. Also, meat cooked on a barbecue can form potentially cancer-causing compounds – the hotter the temperature and the longer the meat cooks, the more compounds produced.

217

DITCH THE DISPOSABLE

Disposable barbecues are a complete waste of resources – they cannot be recycled or composted. For a longer-lasting alternative, try a bucket barbecue, which consists of a galvanized bucket with air holes in the sides and bottom, a wooden handle and removable grill top. Stand on paving or sand, add the sustainable and locally sourced charcoal and you're off!

218

MAKE USE OF THE ASH

Charcoal ash (but not briquette ash) can be used as a fertilizer and will raise the pH of acidic soils, but it's very alkaline and should be applied sparingly. You can also sprinkle a little of the ash around your plants to keep slugs at bay.

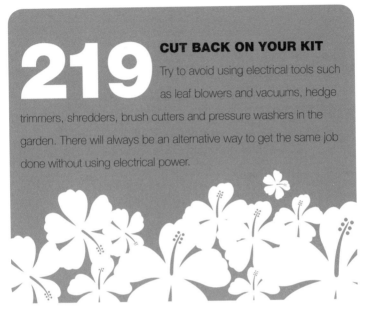

219 CUT BACK ON YOUR KIT

Try to avoid using electrical tools such as leaf blowers and vacuums, hedge trimmers, shredders, brush cutters and pressure washers in the garden. There will always be an alternative way to get the same job done without using electrical power.

220 NO NEED TO HEAT

To be really productive many gardeners heat their greenhouses in the winter months but you may be able to keep it warm enough if you do the following: install your greenhouse below ground level to reduce the chance of frost, insulate it and site it against a wall which will give off the heat absorbed during any sunny days.

221 CREATE A NATURAL SWIMMING POND

For the ultimate in getting back to nature, build a swimming pond in your garden. More than 1,000 natural swimming ponds have been built in Austria, Germany and Switzerland alone. They are a chemical-free combination of swimming area and aquatic plant garden, which are self-cleaning due to the natural cleaning properties of plants.

222 COVER YOUR POOL

If you do have a swimming pool in your back garden, at least make sure you cover it when not in use. This will reduce water loss, prevent heat escaping and ensure it stays as clean as possible, minimizing the need for chemical cleaners and filtration.

223 BE SUN SAFE

Keen gardeners are likely to be exposed to the sun daily for more hours than most other people, so taking precautions against UV exposure is vital. Always wear a wide-brimmed hat and sunglasses with a good-quality UVA blocking filter (an increase in the early formation of cataracts has been linked to prolonged sun exposure). Give natural suncreams based on plant-based ingredients a try. Best of all, spend the hottest part of the day under the shade of a tree.

224 DON'T PLANT SOUVENIRS

In many countries it is illegal to bring plants or seeds from other countries back home with you, but if you do don't plant them in your garden. They are non-native species that might introduce unwanted pests or diseases.

225 BONFIRES ARE BAD

Burning your garden waste is not only a waste of good composting material, it also produces smoke-containing pollutants such as carbon monoxide. And by producing carbon dioxide and heat, it does little to reduce global warming.

226 LOOK FOR CERTIFICATION

When buying wood products for your garden, check they carry either the Forest Stewardship Council (FSC) label or the 'SmartWood Rediscovered' label from the SmartWood's Rediscovered Wood Program, which certifies wood that would otherwise rot, get chipped up or be dumped in a landfill. Sources include dilapidated buildings, 'nuisance' or fallen trees on urban or suburban land and unproductive trees in orchards.

227

TAKE THE PLASTIC BACK

If you can't avoid transporting plants home from a nursery in plastic or polystyrene trays or pots, ask your retailer if you can return them so that they can be reused.

228

EAT YOUR WEEDS

Perhaps this will help encourage you to get on your knees and start pulling them up – some weeds make tasty additions to salads. Try eating varieties such as dandelion, purslane and lamb's quarters when young and tender, but don't pick them at the roadside where they may be affected by dirt and pollution.

229 TRY NATURALISTIC PLANTING

Pioneered in Germany and Holland, this style of planting steers clear of formal borders and plants according to habitat, with the emphasis being on plants developing as they would naturally. This kind of planting requires less regular maintenance and plants are cut back just once a year. See *Planting the Natural Garden* by Piet Oudolf and Henk Gerritsen (Timber Press, 2003).

230 GET SPROUTING

You can grow sprouts in a tray or spare jar but without proper drainage fungi and bacteria may grow, so it might be worth investing in a sprouter that has multiple layers and trays with drainage holes. Make sure you buy organic, non-GM sprout seeds (try your local health food store), which you soak. Mung and radish beans take 12 hours, alfalfa and quinoa 4 hours. Rinse and then grow, remembering to rinse each day. They could be ready to eat in as little as 12 hours for quinoa and 5–6 days for most others.

231 HAVE A PLANT DETOX

Studies have shown that the air quality in our homes could be worse than outdoors due to the prevalence of pollutants such as volatile organic compounds (VOCs) released from upholstery, curtains, plywood, stains and varnishes, paints and carpets. But many common house plants can remove these chemicals from the air. Among 50 house plants tested for their ecological benefits, the areca palm, lady palm, bamboo palm, rubber plant, *Dracaena deremensis* 'Janet Craig', Boston fern and peace lily ranked highly.

232 PLAN AHEAD FOR HALLOWEEN

Grow your own Halloween lanterns as well as enjoying great-tasting soup, pies and cakes. Pumpkins suit warm, sunny conditions with well-drained soil. Sow seed in spring and keep the pumpkins from rotting by placing them on a bed of straw while growing. Once ripe, cut them off with a knife to leave a length of stalk and put outside for ten days in full sun to harden fully.

233 SPENT MUSHROOM COMPOST

This is a waste product from the mushroom-growing industry and it is usually quite inexpensive (to find some, try 'mushroom growers' in your phone directory or online). Being slightly alkaline, it's useful if you need to correct the pH level of the soil and it can also be used as a mulch to help keep down weeds. But you do need to check with the source whether any pesticide residues might be present, particularly organochlorides, which are used against the fungus gnat, or any chemicals.

234 A TREE ISN'T JUST FOR CHRISTMAS

Buy a rooted Christmas tree and you will be able to plant it outdoors at the end of the festive season and (if you keep it in a container) re-use it the following year. Be sure to acclimatize the tree to being outdoors again for a month before planting, and start it off in a sheltered area with some natural light. Gradually move it down the garden to a more exposed area. But beware – Norway spruce grows to 30 m (100 ft).

235 RECYCLE YOUR COMPOST BAGS

Save empty bags of compost or growing media and use them again as grow bags. Fill with homemade compost and flatten them to force air out, then tape or wire the open end shut. Lay flat and make x-shaped holes approximately 45 cm (18 in) apart and water well before planting out tomatoes, lettuces or other seedlings. You can also plant potatoes in them (pierce some drainage holes in the bottom) or use them to line hanging baskets.

236 ADOPT A VEGETABLE

Help save a rare vegetable variety under threat of extinction. Britain's organic growing charity, Garden Organic, looks after over 800 varieties of rare and heirloom vegetables in its heritage seed library (HSL) and offers the chance to adopt one of these vulnerable varieties through its 'Adopt a Veg' scheme. Diversity of varieties means crops are less likely to fall foul of pests and diseases on a massive scale.

237 CHECK ON CACTI

There's a flourishing illegal trade in cacti that is wiping out native populations, particularly from Mexico. Some species are totally banned from international trade and some require an import permit, too. The majority of cacti for sale have been artificially grown in nurseries and are legal, but cacti that are imported into a country do require a permit. If in doubt, check the documentation.

238 INVEST IN PAPER BAGS

You can buy brown paper (grocery) bags online for less than 1p (2 cents) each and they are invaluable in the garden. Store saved seeds in them over the winter, for example, or use them to bag up fruit from your own trees to give to visitors or neighbours. Once used, they can then be added to your compost.

239 MAKE YOUR OWN LOGS

Invest in a logmaker (look out for those made from recycled plastic). They convert newspapers, junk mail, shredded paper, wrapping paper, cardboard, card packaging, dry leaves, wood chips, twigs and sticks, even dried tea bags into fuel logs by compressing and encasing them in newspaper.

240 GROW HERBS ON YOUR WINDOW

Space is no excuse! You can now buy a mini plant-propagator, called the BeanPod, which attaches to windows with a sucker. Inside each bean-shaped pod is a disc of compressed coco-fibre peat that, when watered, expands into enough soil to fill the bottom half of the pod. Sow the seeds provided – basil, chives or parsley – and keep watering. You can even have a herb garden next to your desk at work!

241 CREATE A MULTI-STOREY

Borrow this idea from Africa, where water and fertile land are scarce, particularly in crowded urban areas. Line some old tyres with used plastic bags, fit loose wooden slats along the bottom, allowing room for drainage, and then fill with soil. Use wooden stakes to arrange the tyres in layers – like a wedding cake – and plant crops on each tier. Water from the top down – the loose slats will allow the water to trickle through to each level. Mulch on top of the soil will also help retain moisture.

242 AFTER THE FIZZ HAS GONE

Build your own planters from old drink cans. You will need around 500 to make a 1.5 m (5 ft) diameter planter. Make a cardboard circle template to the above measurement. Fill each can with soil and plug with newspaper. Line up in a single layer along the outer edge of the circle, with bottoms facing out; glue together with waterproof glue. Add another layer on top. Once you have reached about six layers high, slide out the template. Fill the inside space with soil and plant with flowers.

243

USE RECYCLED PLASTIC DECKING

Look out for decking made from recycled plastic – it already accounts for around 10% of the US decking market. It looks good, is low-maintenance and contains no toxic chemicals.

244

UP CLOSE AND PERSONAL

Encourage children to engage with the wildlife in your garden by investing in a solar insect theatre. This consists of an insect viewing chamber made from timber and a solar light that automatically comes on at dusk, attracting moths, lacewings, butterflies and other interesting flying insects into the chamber. The lower shelf also has solitary bee nesting holes.

245 MAKE A HOME FOR THEM

For an earth-friendly approach to controlling slugs, recycle the black packs in which your seedlings or annuals arrive. Place the empty containers upside down near the base of plants. As the plants mature, hide the containers under the leaves. Each morning, check for pests. If you find any, simply empty the container.

246 PLAN AHEAD WITH NEW GARDENS

If you are creating a new garden, you can incorporate water-saving ideas into your plan. For example, if you are on an exposed site consider putting up windbreaks or planting shrubs or hedges to achieve shelter and shade. Use large plants and garden structures, too, to create areas of light shade in exposed, sunny spots.

247

FIT SENSORS

Make sure all your external lights use infra-red sensors (ask your electrician to fit them on existing lights) that are adjusted to come on when you pass in front of them. This will ensure lights operate for the least amount of time necessary.

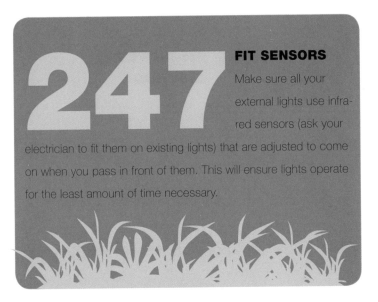

248

DRIP COLLECTION

Take care never to waste water. When watering hanging baskets, put your plant pots or containers below to collect the excess water, which can then be re-routed to other plants or the lawn itself.

249

BEYOND YOUR BACKYARD

There are many opportunities to practise your gardening skills away from the home – contact your local authority to find out about your nearest allotment, set up or join a community group linked to a local park or green space, start a school gardening club, or begin fundraising to create a school garden.

250

BE PROACTIVE

Your support counts! Ask local garden centres and nurseries to stock more native plants, and to stop selling peat and toxic pesticides. Find out how your green spaces are managed and lobby to prevent local authorities from using weed killer and other toxic chemicals. You could also join an environmental, organic gardening or wildlife organization.